NATURAL DISASTERS

The Power of Earthquakes

Susan Bullen

Wayland

Natural Disasters

A Storm Rages
A Volcano Erupts
Flood Damage
The Power of
Earthquakes

Editor: Deb Elliott
Designer: Malcolm Walker

Cover pictures: background – A view of
the San Andreas Fault which runs for 965
kilometres along the coast of California in
the USA. left – A road destroyed by an
earthquake in Hokkaido, Japan. middle –
A firefighter attempts to put out a fire
after the 1989 San Francisco earthquake.
right – Emergency services at work in San
Francisco the day after the Loma Prieta
earthquake.

Text is based on *Earthquake* in *The Violent
Earth* series published in 1992
First published in 1994 by
Wayland (Publishers) Ltd
61, Western Road, Hove
East Sussex, BN3 1JD, England

**British Library Cataloguing in Publication
Data**
Bullen, Susan
  Earthquakes. - (Natural Disasters Series)
  I. Title II. Series
  551.2

ISBN 0 7502 1187 3

Typeset by Kudos
Printed and bound by
  Rotolito Lombarda s.p.a.

Contents

◀   *Earthquakes can turn people's homes into rubble in just a few seconds!*

It's an earthquake!

On 31 May 1970, something frightening happened in the port of Chimbote in Peru. The ground began to tremble. Then there was a loud rumble and buildings shook. It was an earthquake.

This village was ruined by the earthquake. The inset picture shows some people who survived the earthquake. ▶

▼ *Peru is a country in South America.*

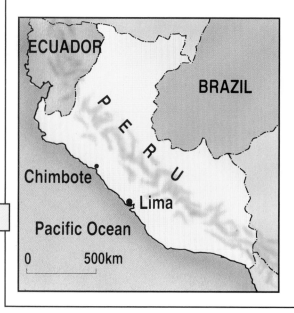

The earthquake was so violent that buildings fell down. Rocks and mudslides came down from the mountains. About 50,000 people were killed in Chimbote and the area around it.

Why do earthquakes happen?

Earthquakes begin deep underground. Right in the core of the Earth it is very hot. In fact, rock around the core melts. On the outside of the Earth, the crust is made of huge plates of rock. They move around slowly above the molten rock.

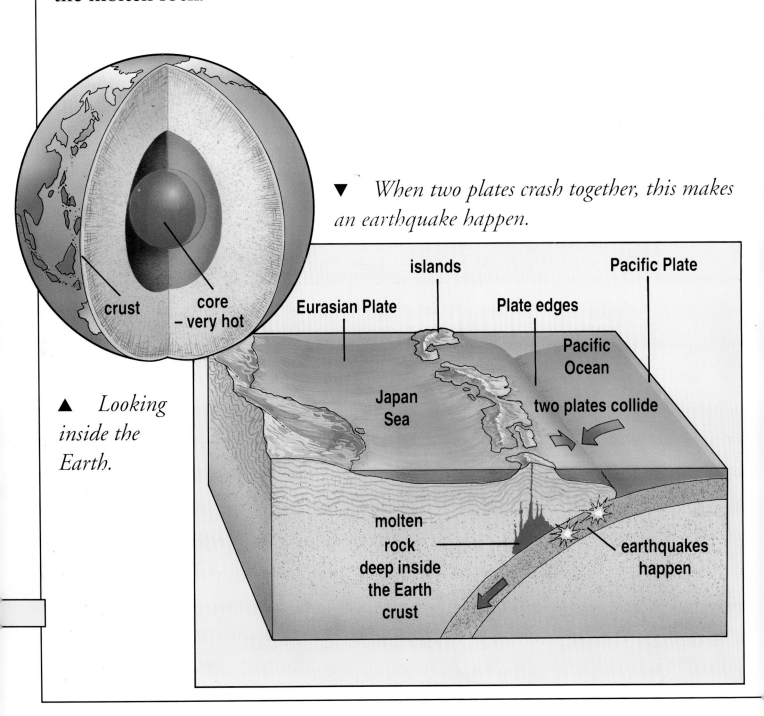

▼ *When two plates crash together, this makes an earthquake happen.*

crust

core – very hot

▲ *Looking inside the Earth.*

islands

Pacific Plate

Eurasian Plate

Plate edges

Pacific Ocean

Japan Sea

two plates collide

molten rock deep inside the Earth crust

earthquakes happen

Sometimes two of the Earth's plates collide as they move around. They break at a weak point and this makes a huge jolt. Then the ground above shakes. This is the earthquake.

How earthquakes happen

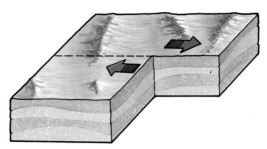

1. Rock is pushed and pulled along a line of weakness.

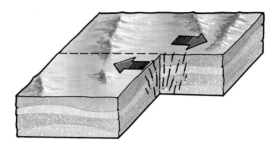

2. Cracks appear in the rock.

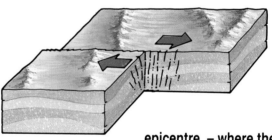

3. The rocks break where they are weak.

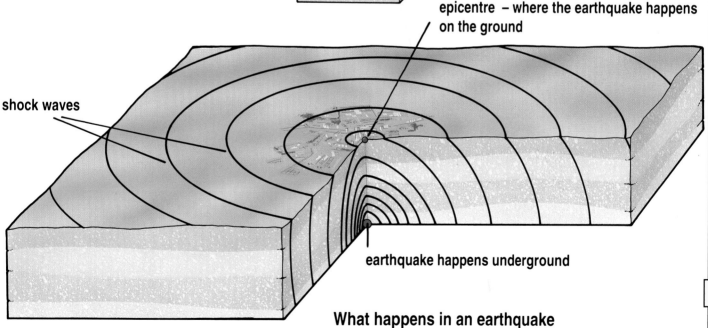

epicentre – where the earthquake happens on the ground

shock waves

earthquake happens underground

What happens in an earthquake

Look at the map below. The blue lines show the edges of the different plates. The red dots show earthquakes. Notice how nearly all earthquakes follow the plate edges.

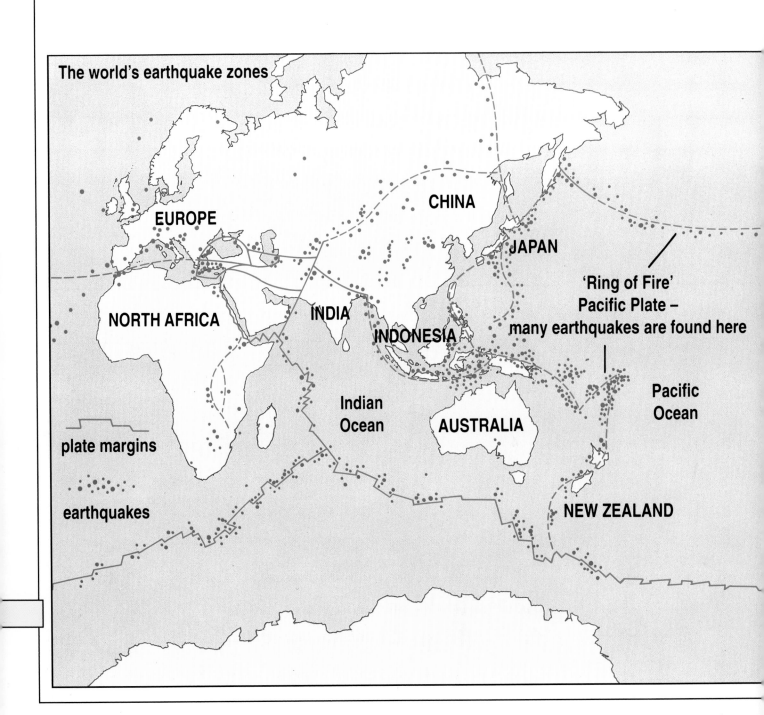

The world's earthquake zones

CHINA

EUROPE

JAPAN

'Ring of Fire'
Pacific Plate –
many earthquakes are found here

NORTH AFRICA

INDIA

INDONESIA

Indian
Ocean

Pacific
Ocean

AUSTRALIA

plate margins

earthquakes

NEW ZEALAND

◄ *Earthquakes happen at the San Andreas Fault in the USA.*

Most earthquakes happen around the Pacific Plate. It can be dangerous near the plate edges.

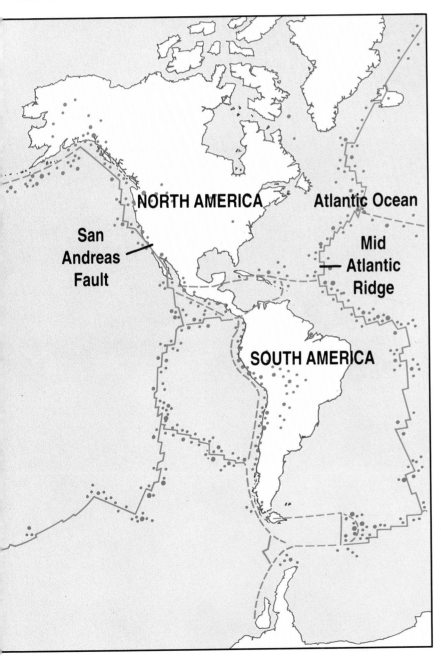

Earthquakes of this century	
Date Place	People killed (in thousands)
1908 Italy	160
1920 China	180
1923 Japan	143
1935 India	60
1938 Turkey	40
1960 Morocco	12
1970 Peru	50
1972 Nicaragua	12
1976 China	700
1976 Guatemala	23
1988 Armenia	55
1990 Iran	35

Powerful earthquakes

Usually, earthquakes last just a few seconds. But they make the ground heave and shake. This can ruin buildings, roads and powerlines.

▼   *An earthquake in Alaska has ripped open the ground and broken up power cables.*

Strength	Point on Richter Scale	Damage
quite mild	4	cracks in walls
stronger	5	some damage to weak buildings
medium	6	most buildings damaged
stronger	7	most buildings destroyed
very strong	8	specially strong buildings damaged
extremely powerful	9	widespread destruction

In the mountains earthquakes can set off enormous landslides. At sea earthquakes sometimes make giant waves. Landslides and giant waves are very dangerous.

▲ *Earthquakes can be mild or very powerful. We measure them on the Richter Scale.*

▼ *Earthquakes can cause landslides and giant waves.*

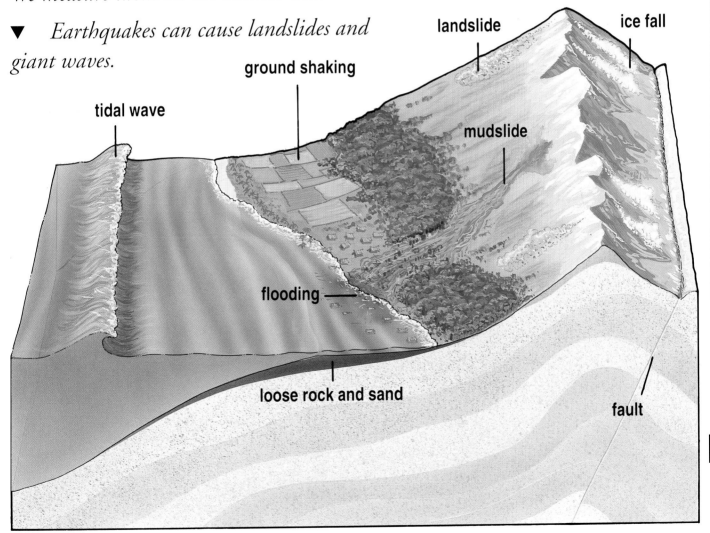

landslide

ice fall

ground shaking

mudslide

tidal wave

flooding

loose rock and sand

fault

Earthquakes of this century

In California, USA, there is a 32-kilometre deep crack inside the Earth's crust. It is called the San Andreas Fault. Below it, two plates are moving in opposite directions. This has caused huge earthquakes.

▼ *San Francisco after the 1906 earthquake.*

A woman described the 1906 earthquake like this: 'I felt sure the house would fall before I got out. It rocked like a ship on a rough sea.'

▲ *This house collapsed in the 1989 earthquake.*

◄ *A newspaper headline about the first earthquake.*

In 1906 a huge earthquake hit San Francisco, in California. It ruined homes, shops and offices and started big fires. About 700 people died and 250,000 lost their homes.

Another earthquake hit San Francisco in 1989. It destroyed homes, roads and bridges and sixty-eight people were killed.

On 19 September 1985, Mexico City was rocked by a huge earthquake. It destroyed about half of this big city.

▼ *Rescue workers look for people trapped in the rubble.*

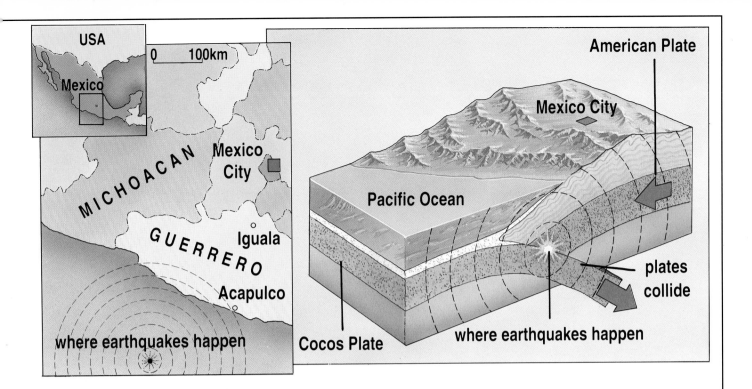

▲ *These maps show Mexico and where the earthquake happened.*

▲ *When two plates collided, the Mexico City earthquake happened.*

Tall buildings, called skyscrapers, tumbled down, leaving rubble everywhere. It was chaos! About 7,000 people were killed and thousands more were injured.

The Mexico City
earthquake measured
8.1 on the Richter Scale.

Another very powerful earthquake happened around the Chinese city of Tangshan. You can see it on this map. ▶

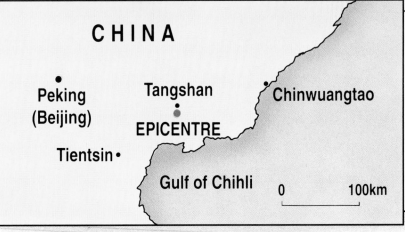

CHINA

Peking (Beijing)

Tangshan

Chinwuangtao

EPICENTRE

Tientsin •

Gulf of Chihli

0   100km

The earthquake happened suddenly on 28 July 1976. The big industrial city of Tangshan was almost completely destroyed and 750,000 people died.

Today Tangshan has been totally rebuilt. The new buildings are much stronger than the old ones. Another earthquake would cause less damage.

◄ *Tangshan looked like this just after the earthquake.*

China's worst earthquakes

Year	Place	People killed
1290	China	100,000
1556	Shensi province	830,000
1731	Peking (Beijing)	100,000
1920	Kansu province	200,000
1976	Tangshan	750,000

One of the world's worst earthquakes hit Armenia near Turkey. It happened on 7 December 1988, during the cold winter. About 55,000 people were killed. Survivors were left homeless. They made fires in the street to keep warm.

▼ *These rescue workers are looking for people among the ruins.*

After the earthquake many other countries helped Armenia. They gave food and warm shelters for the homeless people.

You can see Armenia and where the earthquake struck. ▶

This aeroplane brought shelters for earthquake victims. ▼

When will earthquakes happen?

Most earthquakes happen without warning. Often people cannot escape in time. But sometimes we can detect danger before an earthquake strikes.

▼ *This machine traces the movements that come from inside the Earth.*

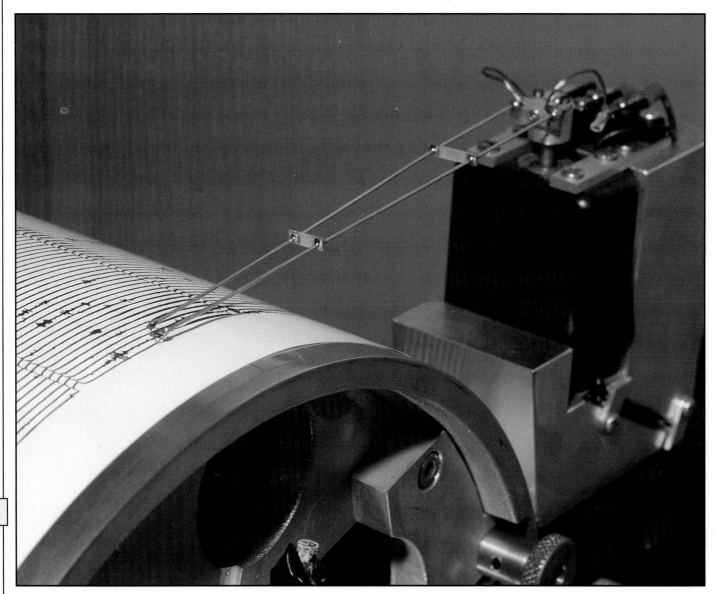

Special machines called seismographs can feel tremors deep in the Earth. If more and more tremors keep happening, this tells us an earthquake may happen soon. These machines have predicted big earthquakes.

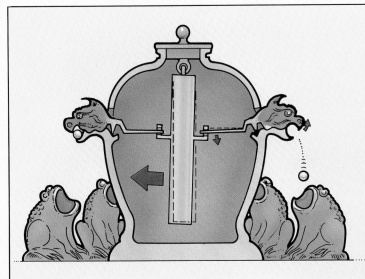

Early earthquake recorder

In the second century, the Chinese made this jar with a pendulum inside. If an earthquake happened, the pendulum moved and knocked a ball. The ball fell from a dragon's mouth into a toad's mouth. Then people could tell where the earthquake came from.

Modern machine

Today, people use a seismograph. This machine picks up movements from the Earth. A pen draws the movements on to a chart.

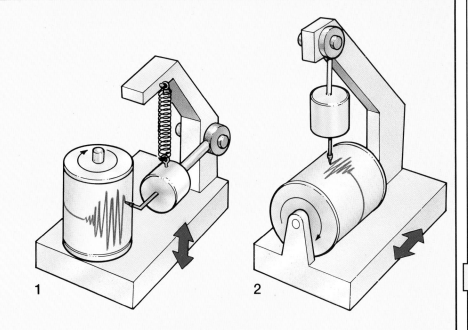

Here are some different ways of testing the ground, to see if there are movements in the Earth. Some methods test the surface. Others go deep underground.

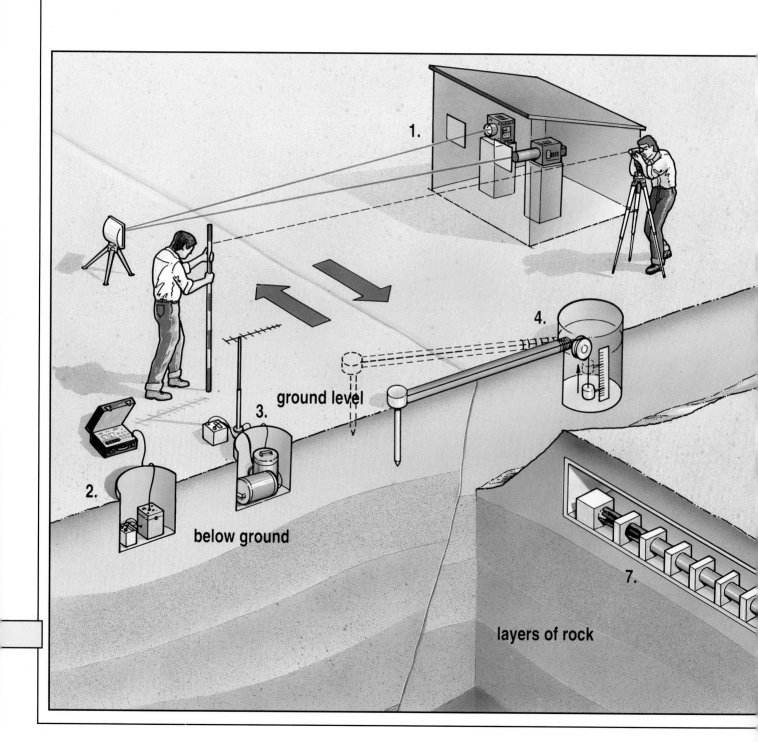

1.

4.

ground level

3.

2.

below ground

7.

layers of rock

There is also a satellite called LAGEOS which helps to predict earthquakes. It spins around above the Earth and uses lasers to see tiny movements in the plates.

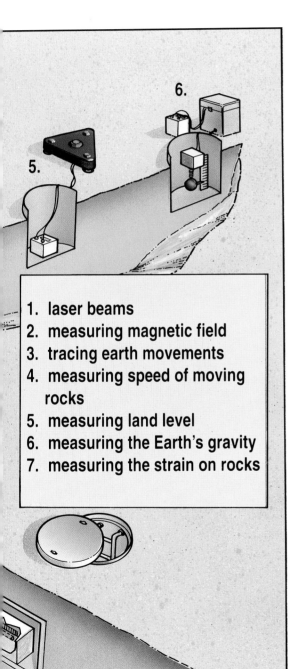

1. laser beams
2. measuring magnetic field
3. tracing earth movements
4. measuring speed of moving rocks
5. measuring land level
6. measuring the Earth's gravity
7. measuring the strain on rocks

▼ *These scientists helped to make the LAGEOS satellite.*

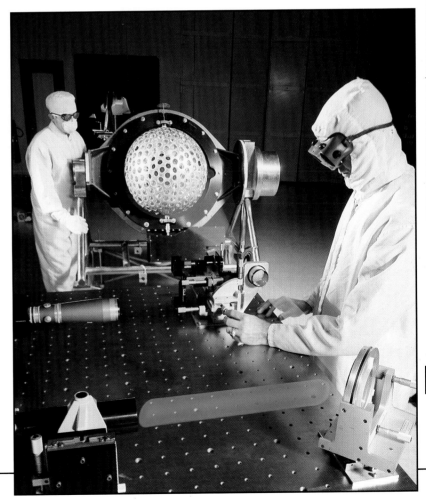

Helping afterwards

Big earthquakes can cause terrible damage. Often people need help after an earthquake has hit their country. So other countries send teams of people with food, clothes, shelter and medicines.

Things to do after an earthquake has struck. ▼

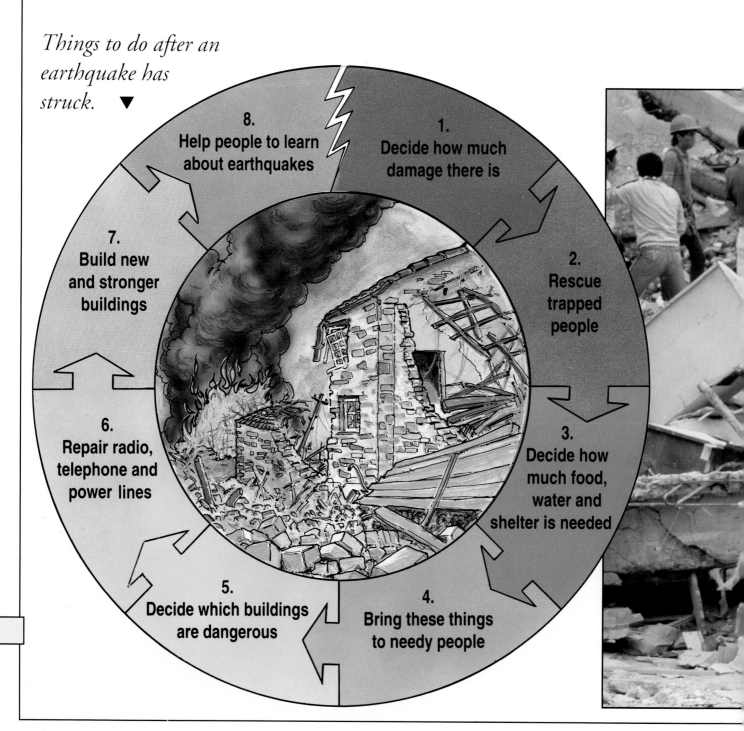

8. Help people to learn about earthquakes

1. Decide how much damage there is

2. Rescue trapped people

3. Decide how much food, water and shelter is needed

4. Bring these things to needy people

5. Decide which buildings are dangerous

6. Repair radio, telephone and power lines

7. Build new and stronger buildings

It takes a long time to return to normal after an earthquake. There is so much rubble to clear up! Then homes must be rebuilt. People must also have electricity, gas and water again.

▼ *These men belong to the international Red Cross rescue team.*

Making places safer

Earthquakes cause less damage if homes are designed to resist them.

▼   *This wooden building soon fell down in an earthquake because its foundations were weak.*

Can you count the floors in these tall buildings?

We can't stop earthquakes happening but we can make buildings safer. New buildings should have very strong foundations.

Skyscrapers can be designed to sway when the ground moves. Then they will not fall down.

◄ *These skyscrapers are built to stay up in an earthquake.*

Projects

Make an earthquake shelter

Ask an adult to help you make this lightweight emergency shelter for victims of an earthquake.

What to do:
1 Draw the four walls of your shelter. Each pair should be the same length.
2 Cut out the rectangles and stick them together.
3 Draw on windows and doors.
4 Cut pieces of drinking straws to make water pipes. Stick them on to your shelter.

You need:
cereal boxes   sticky tape
paper and a pencil
scissors   paper fasteners
glue   drinking straws

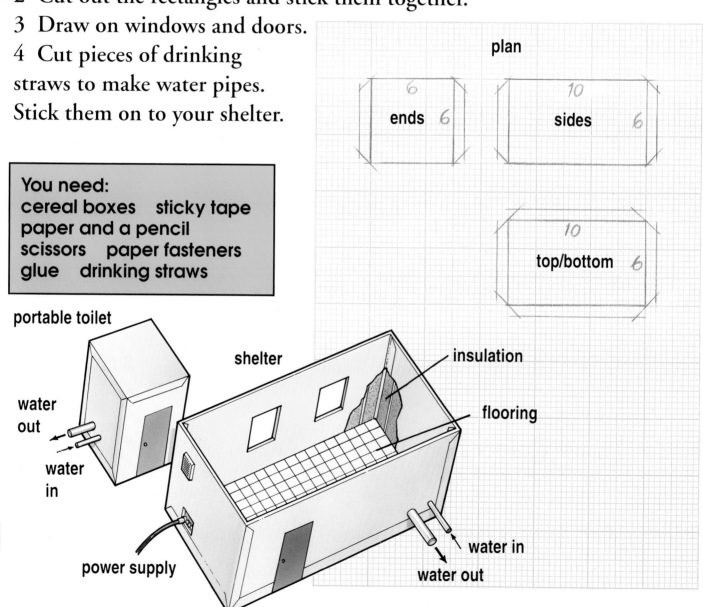

plan

ends   6   6

sides   10   6

top/bottom   10   6

portable toilet

shelter

insulation

flooring

water out

water in

water in

water out

power supply

Make a lightweight house for an earthquake zone

In places where earthquakes happen, lightweight buildings are more likely to stay up.

What to do:

1 Cut the four walls out of the card.

2 Cut the straws to the same length as the walls. Stick them on to the base board.

3 Glue tissue paper on to the wall pieces. Now stick the walls on to the straw square - the foundations.

4 Make the roof from a large piece of card. Score it down the centre. Stick it on top of the walls.

You need:
straws
glue
thin card
tissue paper
sticky tape
pin board and pins

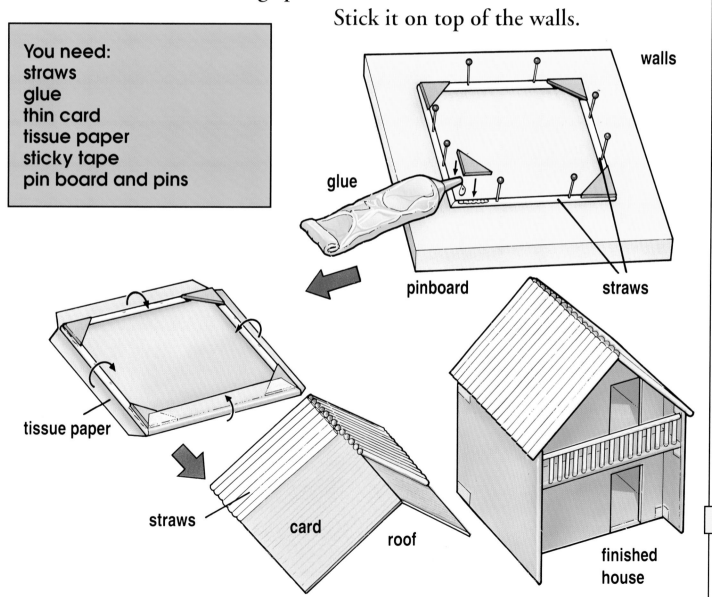

walls

glue

pinboard

straws

tissue paper

straws

card

roof

finished house

Glossary

chaos   When everything is in a mess.

collide   Crash together.

core   The centre of the Earth.

crust   The surface of the Earth, with land and sea on top.

fault   A very deep crack in the Earth's crust.

foundations   The underground base of a building.

laser   A very strong beam of light.

molten   Melted into a liquid.

pendulum   A hanging weight that swings.

predict   Say what will happen in the future.

rescue workers   People who save other people from danger.

rubble   A mass of fallen-down buildings.

satellite   An instrument that travels around our planet, high up in space.

tremors   Slight movements in the ground.

violent   Very powerful and frightening.

Books to read

Earthquake by Brian Knapp
  (Macmillan, 1989)
Natural Disasters by Tim Wood
  (Wayland, 1993)
The San Francisco Earthquake by John
  Dudman (Wayland, 1988)

Picture acknowledgements
The publisher would like to thank the following
for allowing their photographs to be reproduced in
this book: Associated Press/Topham 19 (right);
Colorific! 14 (Alon Reininger/Contact), 24/25
(Frank Fournier/Contact); Frank Lane Picture
Agency 10; Photri 12, 13, 23, 27; Picturepoint Ltd
4/5 (both); Science Photo Library cover, back
ground (David Parker), cover, right (Peter Menzel),
2/3 (Peter Menzel), 9 (David Parker), 20 (Tom
McHugh), 26 bottom (Peter Menzel); Frank
Spooner Pictures Ltd 16/17, 18, 19. All artwork by
Nick Hawken.

Index